CHARACTER FLAW

RENARD PRESS — PLAYSCRIPT XI

CHARACTER FLAW: FIRST PERFORMED AT EDINBURGH FRINGE IN 2023, DIRECTED BY NAT KENNEDY. PIP PLAYED BY PHILIPPA DAWSON, JEAN VOICEOVER BY CHARLY CLIVE, TRAIN TANNOYS / AMY / WOMAN ON TRAIN VOICEOVERS BY HELEN COLBY, TRAIN CONDUCTOR VOICEOVER BY SAMUEL WIGHTMAN AND HS2 ANNOUNCEMENT VOICEOVER BY MATT PENMAN.

CHARACTER FLAW

PHILIPPA DAWSON

RENARD PRESS

RENARD PRESS LTD

124 City Road
London EC1V 2NX
United Kingdom
info@renardpress.com
020 8050 2928

www.renardpress.com

Character Flaw first published by Renard Press Ltd in 2024

Printed on FSC-accredited papers in the UK by 4edge Limited

ISBN: 978-1-80447-134-0

9 8 7 6 5 4 3 2 1

Renard Press is proud to be a climate positive publisher, removing more carbon from the air than we emit and planting a small forest. For more information see renardpress.com/eco.

CHARACTER FLAW

…or is it an ADHD thing?

For my mother.

NOTE

All of the characters will be played by the same actor, unless stated as a voice over. When PIP'S *name is in **bold** she is speaking as herself in the moment; when in* roman *she is speaking to a voiceover, in a sketch or in the past.*

Music builds, drum roll, lights come up on an empty stage. There is a single chair centre stage. Depending on venue, location or times of performance, PIP *could have a different reason for being late – usually relating to having lost her phone, i.e. she got lost, didn't realise the time or couldn't open the door to the theatre as the code was saved on there.*

PIP (*offstage*): Shit! Sorry. (*Noise from offstage.*) I'm coming.

(PIP *enters, wearing a large backpack and carrying a holdall on one arm. Both bags are filled with props. She has headphones around her neck.*)

> Hi, hello everyone. Sorry about that! I wrote the code to the door on my phone and I seem to have lost it! But thank you so much for coming. I'm Pip, by the way. I'm not usually late to my own show. I just (*looking for phone in holdall and backpack*) can't find my… I'm sure it should be in here if I… maybe at the bottom of… AHH! (PIP *pulls out a cucumber, then quickly hides it.*) Never mind. I don't need it for the show. Anyway, this isn't how we were meant to start. It was supposed to be this big grand opening and…

> (*To the technician:*) Do we have time? Yeah? OK.

(*Back to the audience:*) Right. Shall we start again? Amazing! OK, if you can all go (*mimics clapping hands*) 'woooooo' towards the end of the drum roll.

OK, Brian, whenever you're ready!

(PIP *exits. Drum roll.* PIP *enters.*)

Hello! Hello, everyone, thank you so much for coming. My name is Pip and… (*Pause.*) Has anyone here ever lost their phone?

Or maybe left their keys at home?

What about leaving something on a bus? (*Removes headphones.*) Your headphones? Your bag? A water bottle? A passport? Has anyone ever left their passport on a New York City bus three days before your flight home to the UK, so had to travel to the bowels of Brooklyn to retrieve it from a bus depot in the middle of nowhere, only to lose it again three days later when you get back to London?

No? OK, has anyone else ever been bored at work and written a pretend but very offensive resignation letter to their boss, then without realising sent it to the office email?

Or when your mum picked you up from school, and you got in the car, put your bag down, put your seat belt on… did you ever look up and realise it wasn't your mum?

Or have you ever not been paying attention when someone said they had a severe nut allergy, and fed them peanut-butter ice cream?

When something terrible happens, do you instantly panic because you know it will be because of something you've done, you just don't know what that was?

(*Game-show music and colourful lights. Puts on coat and glasses.*)

DOCTOR: Hello, hello! Hi. My name's Doctor Acorno, and I'm gonna be your host today. I'm here to present to you – Attention Deficit Hyperactivity Disorder.

(*Aside:*) Something in the business we call ADHD.

Now, here's where it gets interesting. There are two types of this disorder – inattentive and hyperactive. Some people have one, some people have the other... but from everything we've seen here today, I can confirm this lady suffers from (*drum roll*) the Combined Type!

PIP: The doctor's room smelt like popcorn. I couldn't pay attention. I just stared at a framed poster on the wall showing a girl with clouds around her head. (*Laughs.*) Is that supposed to be ADHD? Is that supposed to be me?

(*Pause.*)

Oh my god, is that supposed to be me?

PIP: Sorry what did you say? I've got ADHD?!

PIP: I was quite overwhelmed that day. In fact, I was quite angry. And sad. I felt quite stupid, and silly. Like I felt nervous and embarrassed and excited and, actually, I did feel really excited.

You see, my whole life I've been told my head is in the clouds. I always felt like there was something wrong with me, because everyone just got things and I couldn't. Like I didn't have the rule book, so I was always playing catch-up and I always felt stupid and silly and... (*Pulls out a textbook from her bag and shows it to the audience.*)

Now I'm being told there is a medical reason for it?!

It says that... Actually... (*Closes book.*) Some of you here probably have ADHD.

If not, you've at least seen a video online with a woman going...

(*Music plays, as though in a TikTok video.*)

TIKTOK VOICEOVER: Positive things I didn't know about ADHD...

(PIP *points to bits of the air around her in the style of a TikTok video, as though text is appearing around her. Music stops.*)

PIP: Soo, instead of doing that, I'll just tell you how ADHD feels for me… Have you ever lost your train of thought?

Well, I don't have a train.

Oh sorry, I should have been more clear. I don't have *a* train. I have a multitude of trains in a very complex railway network, so I don't ever 'lose my train of thought', it just gets taken over by a different one. Because they're all going in different directions, through different stations and different countries. There are even different types of trains!

There are some beautiful old steam trains, those posh Virgin Atlantic trains, and some quite rusty freight trains. There's Crossrail, Scotrail, Thameslink, the First Great Western, the Metro, the Eurostar, the Subway, the underground, the overground, DLR, high-speed trains, commuter trains, Greater Anglia, the Caledonian Sleeper, the Trans-Siberian Railway, the Orient Express, the Gatwick Express, the Heathrow Express, the Chiltern Express, the Stansted Express, the Hogwarts Express, the Polar Express and Thomas the Tank Engine!

(*Toot toot sound.*)

But *every* single train is—

TRAIN TANNOY VOICEOVER: …experiencing delays because of a signal failure.

PIP: I also have anxiety. And a simple way I can describe this to you is – imagine I'm travelling on every single one of those trains. Well, now imagine that I've dodged buying a ticket for every single one of those trains. So on some I'm trying to look asleep, on another I'm hiding in the toilet, on one I've unpacked all my belongings to make it look like I've been there for hours. But on most of the trains I'm just sitting, looking over my shoulder, trying to fit in and hoping I don't get found out.

(*Slight pause.* PIP *puts textbooks on the chair. Stands with clipboard as if in front of school noticeboard.*)

MR TILLY: The Supreme Court's influence over the policy-making processes are of ultra-significance...

PIP: This is Mr Tilly, my A-level politics teacher. He's passionate about Karl Marx, socialism, the environment, women's rights, gay rights, equal rights, period poverty, the NHS, and one time he brought in two different types of chocolate cake to illustrate the different political voting systems.

I don't remember what it meant but—

MR TILLY: PIP! Are you paying attention?

PIP: I hate lying to him, but I can't tell him that instead of writing notes on legislative processes I'm actually composing a list of things to do before I die. Not big things like climbing Everest, just the small things like learn to solve a Rubik's cube, shave my head, run the Stratford-upon-Avon marathon, have sex on a plane, have sex up a tree, fall out of a tree, have six children, save someone's life, order a 'coffee to go', make out with a girl, hitch-hike to Scotland, get a tattoo and be a maid at Buckingham Palace—

MR TILLY: And why do you keep shuffling about on your chair?

PIP (*pulling out textbooks from underneath her*): I'm just sitting on a pile of books. I genuinely thought if I made myself uncomfortable I wouldn't be able to daydream.

MR TILLY: Well it's clearly not working. I know, I know. For the rest of the lesson you can stand up here, next to me, and do your work on the board. That way you won't be able to daydream, because the whole class will be watching you.

(PIP *stands in front of the board, trying to concentrate.*)

PIP: Well, it obviously didn't work.

My school reports were filled with 'could try harder', 'she tends to drift away' and 'Philippa seems to prefer talking to her classmates than doing her work'.

My maths teacher told the boy sitting behind me that every time I stopped paying attention he should poke me with a sharp compass.

Why was it easier for teachers to encourage bullying than consider that I might have a problem?

(*Reading from textbook:*) 'Symptoms of Attention Deficit Hyperactivity Disorder in girls and those assigned female at birth are often seen as character flaws.'

Great. I was annoying but… not socially disruptive, so no one did anything about it.

And this word 'Deficit' is doing wonders for my self-esteem…

TRAIN TANNOY: Your attention please. (*Fades out.*) This is a…

PIP: Attention Deficit? Attention Deficit?

(*Trying to lighten the word:*) Deeeficit. DefiCIT? De Fi Cit… Deficit?

DEFICIT.

(*Slight pause.*)

I've fixated on this word. It's horrible. It implies that there's something lacking. A shortfall in my mind. Nothing there.

(*With each word the stage grows darker, until* PIP *is left sitting in darkness.*)

Deficit. Empty. Barron. Hollow. Void. Derelict. Inadequate.

(*Silence.*)

JEAN: Helllooooo? Is anyone there?

PIP: Hey.

JEAN (*banging into filing cabinet*): OW! Why is it so dark in here?

PIP: I'm just feeling really sad. About my empty head.

JEAN: Ohhhh, don't be so dramatic in front of these nice people. Let me find that switch... (*Hums.*) Ah, here we are. (*Click. Lights on.*) Oh my dear lord. Empty?! Empty?!?! I've never seen so many filing cabinets in my life! (*Rummaging through drawers.*) What is all this rubbish?

PIP: This is Jean, by the way. She lives in my head, and she's always having a clear-out.

(*Work setting.* PIP *picks up computer keyboard and begins to type.*)

JEAN: Dear, I've noticed all of the science folders are filled with photos of pop stars!

PIP: Oh, don't worry about those files.

JEAN: Oh my goodness! Did you do anything in physics other than think about Hanson?

PIP: Oh, they did have great hair though they looked like girls... No, Jean, please don't distract me. I'm at work.

JEAN: Well, these archives are a complete mess. Nothing makes sense! I just saw a story about a—

PIP: Jean! My boss is in the office today. I cannot be thinking about... *Sugar Rush*? Why are you thinking about—

JEAN: Well, I'm just looking in the geography files, and there are a lot of odd things in here. Who is Miss Lambert?

PIP (*blushing*): Oh, she was just my geography teacher.

JEAN: Well, you have got a lot of stories about her...

Oh my!

Did you do any work in geography, dear? I'm only seeing things about her

PIP: Well, she was an important part of my education.

JEAN: I think some of these stories aren't true, dear. I don't think you and her were ever stuck in a lift together, and I highly doubt she invited you back to her house to watch *Sugar Rush*—

PIP: Oh, Jean, please don't look at that memory! It's more of a fantasy—

JEAN: Oh, my dear, she's your teacher – that is very unprofessional...

PIP: Jean, please stop looking at that—

JEAN: MY DEAR GIRL, YOU'RE... OH, MY EYES!

PIP: JEAN!!!! That's PRIVATE!!! Shit, Jean, my boss is coming over. She looks like she's been crying.

(*To boss:*) Hi Amy!

AMY: Hi, Pip. I need to leave the office for a bit. I've just had some terrible news.

JEAN: She's got such good posture – I wonder if she—

PIP (*to* JEAN): Shh!

(*To* AMY:) Is everything OK?

AMY: Not really, no. Are you OK to hold the fort?

PIP: Hold the fort?

(*As* AMY *tells* PIP *the story about her cat,* JEAN *talks at the same time.* PIP *tries to look like she is listening to* AMY, *but isn't able to listen and misses the important details.*)

JEAN (JEAN *and* AMY*'s voiceovers play over each other*): Hold the fort, eh? That's an interesting idiom. It must have come from one of the wars. I suppose it's up there with telling someone to choose your battles, or to take a shot in the dark! She was armed to the teeth, but caught in the crossfire. You must stick to your guns... because all's fair in love and war...

AMY: Yeah, I just need to go home. My neighbour called and apparently a cat has been found on the road. She looks like Sultan – Sultan's my cat. But they aren't sure it's her because of all the blood. They said the blood made her look golden, but she is actually a white cat. God, I'm so worried – it can't be my cat, can it? She can't be dead... my cat never crosses the road. It must be a different cat – what do you think? Do you think my cat is dead?

PIP (*laughing, unaware of what* AMY *has said*): Yes. Annoying. OK, see you tomorrow.

(*To* JEAN:) What was she saying about her cat? Oh my god, I wasn't listening!

JEAN: Well, it's not your fault dear. There was a lot going on at the same time with all those wartime phrases and analogies.

PIP: Shhhh!

(*Slight pause.*)

PIP: When Jean finds a story, I can't control the impulse to start thinking about it. Or interrupt someone and say it. It's why I can't control an impulse to jump on a bus without checking the number, or shout out something really personal at a comedy gig, or sign up to do the Stratford-upon-Avon marathon when I don't like running but I saw it on an advert on TV and remembered I'd written it on a to-do list when I was sixteen.

Sometimes it's impossible to weed out the different—

JEAN: OWWW we know about weeds! Tell them about the garden!

PIP: Oh, well I was in the middle of—

JEAN: Tell them!

PIP: When I moved to London, I started applying for all sorts of small and very random jobs.

(*As* PIP *tells the story she pulls out various props to set the scene. A cucumber is used as a lawnmower handle.*)

One lady was looking for someone to water her garden, look after her vegetables and mow the lawn. I accepted the job straight away, even though I'd never mowed a lawn in my life. I was assuming she wouldn't see me do it... but she did. She actually sat there and watched me the whole time! I suddenly wondered if I'd applied to a different sort of job, and perhaps I should have worn something different and charged a bit more.

Well, she obviously saw something she liked, and asked me to go back each week.

She'd also asked me to cover everything in insect killer. She said (PIP *puts on sultry, husky voice and leans back in the chair*) 'until they're dripping' – which I thought was a bit intense.

'Slugs are rife, darling, I need you to be my little warrior.'

(*Mouthing:*) OH MY GOD.

I ran to that shed.

I grabbed that bottle. (*Holds bottle like a gun,* Charlie's Angels *style.*)

And I went for it!

I covered the garden, until it was, as she had asked, dripping. (*Blows away pretend gun smoke.*)

I went back to the shed, and saw she had a second bottle of insect killer. OK.

Then I started to feel a bit sick, and I looked in my hands, at the bottle that I had used.

It wasn't insect killer.

I had drenched her entire, beautiful garden in weed killer.

But then I thought it's fine, it's fine. Weed killer is just for weeds, isn't it. So it'll only kill the weeds. Then I realised chemicals don't understand the social status of plants, and it would kill everything in its tracks! I asked Google and they said:

NERDY GOOGLE TECH VOICE (PIP): Oh. Well. This is a disaster, and your only option is to wash the garden.

PIP: WASH THE GARDEN.

To make things worse she only had a watering can!

(PIP *puts on backpack.*)

TRAIN TANNOY: The train now approaching platform six is the 09:32 service to Bristol Temple Meads.

PIP: SIX?? No, I thought it said nine! (*Takes off backpack.*)

PIP: I'm dyslexic as well. Although they discovered that one when I was in school…

JEAN: Do you remember your first day in school, when the netball teacher asked what it's called when you move in front of someone to catch the ball?

PIP: Oh yes, I do. Interception. (*Demonstrating to the audience.*) In netball it's called interception!

JEAN: But you said Contraception. (*Cracking up.*) Oh, you were so excited that you knew the answer – you were only eleven, and you proudly shouted it out in front of the whole class. CONTRACEPTION!!

PIP: Thanks. I made a lot of embarrassing mistakes in school, and I never felt like I fitted in.

Until I discovered… 'The Dramatic Arts!'

Even in primary school, when I was cast as (*acts out strange wave-like movements*) 'a bit of the ocean', I was really happy. But in secondary school, when I was cast as Second Ukulele… Even though I couldn't play the ukulele. And… (*pulling ukulele from backpack*) full disclosure, I still can't play the ukulele. It didn't matter. Because I finally felt like I fitted in. I'd found my place! And dyslexia wasn't ever getting in my way!

DYSLEXIA SONG

PIP *starts playing one note, and begins to sing slowly. As the playing becomes louder and more dramatic, so does* PIP *'s singing and movements. The last verse is almost like a dramatic finale from a musical or rock concert.*

Back when I was younger I was struggling in school.
They said I had dyslexia, cause I couldn't spell at all.
They moved me into special needs… (*spoken:*) SO uncool!
They said, 'Dyslexia's not scary… we have posters on the wall.'

They taught me how to see each letter;
Reading was so much better,
And surely this new learning plan
Would help my short attention span!

Yes, surely this new learning plan
Would help my short attention span!

SURELY this new learning plan
Would help my short attention span?

(*spoken:*) It's didn't.
And now they say it's ADHD and I'm attention deficit,
My learning difficulties become a disorder and I have to admit

I miss just being dyslexic,
And every special-needs game
When my teacher gave me extra time,
But now life isn't the same.

(*Sings:*)
Attention Deficit Hyperactivity Disorder.
Please don't judge me, this sounds serious,
It's not just about word order;
I miss the days when I was younger.
Naïve and innocent,
I was happy.
Life was simple.
When dyslexia was sexier.

PIP: When they discover you have dyslexia they give you all these learning tools and new equipment. They did this all over again for ADHD when I went to uni. To be honest, it was a lot of technology that was far too complicated for my attention span, but one tool I really do remember. It plugged into the computers at uni and read out loud everything you typed.

(She sits down as if at a computer. In this section PIP *is typing each line on a computer keyboard, and we hear the automated and computerised male voiceover reading each line aloud.* PIP *types 'hello'.)*

COMPUTER VOICEOVER: Hello.

This is the computer speaking.

Did you hear the gossip? I hope I haven't got my wires crossed. But I've heard the printer's been having it off with the Wi-Fi.

There was a strong connection.

She was going to unzip his files when she realised the keyboard was more her type.

PIP: Lunchtime had just started and the computer room was filling up, so I had to stop. I put my headphones on and started messaging a friend instead.

(PIP *begins typing to her friend, but the voiceover continues reading aloud through the computer.* PIP*'s headphones aren't plugged in, and she doesn't notice.*)

COMPUTER VOICEOVER: Hey!

You should have stayed longer at Dalston Superstore – you know the girl who looked like Margot Robbie? Oh god, she was actually so hot, I can't believe she fancied me too.

PIP (*removing headphones and talking to the audience*): I often wonder if ADHD gives you paranoia – I swear everyone in the computer room was looking at me.

(*Replaces headphones and goes back to typing.*)

COMPUTER VOICEOVER: OMG. We kissed. It was SO-O-O-O-O sexy. I was leaving, and I'd given her my number, and then she followed me out, and pushed me up against the wall and, fuck, I was on fire, and she put her hand in my pants and she put her fingers on my...

PIP (*to computer room*): What is everyone staring at?!

(PIP *realises her headphones weren't plugged in.*)

PIP: ADHD has always been outing me – although it did keep me in the closet for a long time.

25

I would date boys, but when I grew bored very quickly or got distracted in the middle of having sex and asked them what the time was… I assumed it was just my short attention span. And when I'd daydream about a woman, sneak off to a gay bar and kiss a girl, or have a secret six-week fling with a woman from work… I'd just put it down to my impulsive tendencies and never think of it again.

It's really sad, though.

Why didn't I take myself seriously?

Why couldn't I listen to myself, recognise what was going on, and then proudly declare…

I'M A LESBIAN!

People would just say, 'Oh, she's a joker!'

(*To self, while scanning textbook:*) Why couldn't I be confident about it? Ah!

(*Reading from book:*) 'Women with ADHD in particular suffer from low self-esteem and rejection-sensitive dysphoria. This is an intense fear of criticism, perceived failure or rejection.' Yeah. (*Puts book down.*)

I'll exhaust myself trying to be the funny one. I won't talk about how I'm actually feeling, because I have this crippling fear that if people don't find me funny…

they'll get bored and they'll hate me. It's like I'm in a bath and—

JEAN: OHHH, tell them the story about the bath!

PIP: No, Jean! I'm actually in the middle of sharing something quite serious and personal with them—

JEAN: Nooo, noo, this is far more important. No one wants to hear something serious and personal, anyway. They'll get bored. And they'll hate you.

(PIP *jumps up and starts to get more belongings out of her bag to 'set the scene'.*)

PIP: So, the other day, about seven years ago, I was house-sitting in a friend's family home. A charming little cottage in the Cotswolds, and I was on my best behaviour, as I have quite a bad track record in other peoples' homes.

That evening I was having a bath. But I couldn't work out how to turn the hot water on and, rather than risk breaking their boiler, I decided to be a martyr and have a cold bath.

I should also mention at this point that I'd just ran 26.2 miles in the Stratford-upon-Avon marathon with little to no training. So I was at peak exhaustion, and thought, whilst the taps were running, some self-care was in order.

(*Turns on music, sits down. A short time passes and* PIP *falls asleep.* PIP *gasps and suddenly realises the taps are still on and runs to turn them off.*)

OH MY GOD! OH MY GOD... Oh my god? It was fine. I had been asleep for over half an hour and the taps had been on! Where did the water go? What is this sorcery? No, I think it just went in that little overflow valve. (*Shrugs.*) So anyway, I had a long, cold bath. During which time my head borderline froze. And then some weird things happened. The music started skipping, and then stopped. Then all the lights went out, and there was a strange sound coming from downstairs.

But I just thought it was a power cut. C'est la vie. I was feeling relaxed and went downstairs.

Now, when I think back to this moment it's sort of in slow motion. I walked into the sitting room and the first thing I saw was my bottle of Cider on the coffee table. It was covered in large droplets of water.

But I just thought it was some really intense condensation.

So I took a step forward on to the thick, luxurious, shaggy carpet and my foot... splashed. And as the picture zoomed out I realised it wasn't just the cider that was covered in water. EVERYTHING WAS COVERED IN WATER. And water was in fact still coming down from the ceiling. And judging by the amount of water in the sitting room, at peak 'bathwater going into the overflow valve' moment, it must have been pouring down!

(PIP *starts pulling the carpet up, drying things, etc.*)

Everything was soaked! I had to pull back the carpet, I had to pull back the underlay... I ran out of towels! (PIP *drops the towel wrapped around her.*) This was all still in the dark, by the way, because water had got into the fuse box.

(*Whilst drying the floor:*) I was exhausted. Especially because I HAD JUST RUN THE MARATHON! And now I was having to scrub the floor, by torchlight, naked! And that's when I saw it. A large, old book that I suddenly remembered my friend's grandmother had been telling me about the night before.

MRS MAYHEWS (PIP): This is the Mayhews' family Bible. It's been passed down in our family for generations. In the front two pages are the births, and the deaths, of our entire family. It's priceless, you see – it goes back four hundred years!

PIP: I'm going to hell.

TRAIN CONDUCTOR: Tickets, please.

PIP: Where are we?

TRAIN CONDUCTOR: We're just coming up into Haywards Heath, love.

PIP: Hampstead Heath?

TRAIN CONDUCTOR: Haywards Heath. We'll get into Brighton in fifteen minutes.

PIP: Brighton? No, I'm on the Hereford train.

TRAIN CONDUCTOR: Hereford? Darlin', that's in the other direction. Have you been on the wrong train since London? You didn't notice you were on the wrong train for an hour? You gotta pay attention. Where's your original train ticket?

PIP: My ticket? I…

(PIP *doesn't have a ticket.*)

PIP: I'm so fed up with trains, so at thirty-three years old, I'm finally learning to drive.

I'm not sure which is worse – crying on a train? Or crying in a car?

(PIP *is now sitting in a car holding the steering wheel.*)

PIP: Why is this so hard?

JEAN: Well, it's not your fault dear.

PIP: I know. I just wish my teacher understood ADHD.

JEAN: Ohhh!

PIP: Ohhh! You're right! I should be a driving teacher for people with ADHD. (*Gasps.*) I could open a driving school just for people with ADHD. It could be called the Neurodrivers and—

JAMIL (*driving teacher*): Are you paying attention?

PIP: Yes, sorry.

JAMIL: If you cannot listen, you will fail your test. We're turning left here.

PIP: OK

Sloooow down. No! Check my mirrors first.

Then slooooow down.

Indicate left. (*Holds up hands in L shapes to find left.*)

Move down a gear...

Foot off the clutch. On to the accelerator.

Check if it's clear.

Slowly. Moving. Forward. Turning and...

I DID IT! Did you see that? Did *you* see that? I turned the car on to a main road—

JAMIL: MOVE! You can't just stop on a main road!

PIP: Oh my god! This is exhausting. I'm going back to the trains.

(PIP *sits back down.*)

TRAIN TANNOY: Good afternoon, and thank you for travelling with us today on Cross Country trains. This train will shortly be arriving into Bristol Temple Meads. For trains going to Bath Spa please note that...

JEAN: OH! Tell them the story about the bath!

PIP: What? I *just* told them the story about the bath. Please don't make me repeat myself in front of all these people—

JEAN: No, no, the *other* story about the bath.

PIP: Which story? Oh!

PIP: About eight years ago I was living in New York City. While I was there I was cat-sitting in this beautiful downtown apartment.

The bathroom was so big there was a roll-top bath in the middle of the room! So, my first evening... The lights were low. The water had been run and the taps were off this time. And I was naked. And I was about to get in when I saw the cat was itching. And then I saw a flea.

(*Putting on coat:*) And I hate fleas. When you see one, there's probably a hundred. They're probably everywhere. So I ran to the shop for flea drops and flea spray for the carpets.

(*Sprays.*) Wow. (*Sprays again.*) It was like smoke. (*Spraying lots more.*) I got very carried away.

(*Smoke machine turns on.*)

Smoke started filling the room.

And then I was naked. (*Drops coat.*)

(*Blackout. Ibiza club music plays. Lights flash on and off showing* PIP *holding various dance poses in the smoke and then jumping as if in a club. Fire alarm sound plays. After five seconds the music stops and* PIP *realises the music she has been dancing to is actually the fire alarm.* PIP *starts fanning the alarm with the towel until it stops.*)

PHEW. Thank god they don't have sprinklers – I cannot flood another house.

Why isn't her cat moving?!

(*Blackout. Lights up.* PIP *puts on backpack and walks up and down a train platform, listening to announcements and background noise, looking increasingly flustered.*)

TRAIN TANNOY: Your attention please. We are sorry to announce that the 11.35 Arriva Trains Wales service to Newport has been cancelled.

PIP: Oh, what?

TRAIN TANNOY: The next train to arrive on platform seven will now be the 11:52 First Great Western service to Reading.

PIP: Reading? Then where does the Swansea train go from?

TRAIN TANNOY: Anyone travelling with an off-peak ticket will have to purchase a new ticket. Off-peak tickets are not valid on this service.

PIP: But that's what I have!

Oh god. This is the worst day of my life.

TRAIN TANNOY: This is a safety announcement. Due to today's wet weather, please take extra care whilst on the station. Surfaces may be slippery.

PIP: Oh my god!

Oh, hi, sorry, I'm really confused – I'm trying to get to Carmarthen and—

TRAIN TANNOY: Please stand well away from the edge of platform seven. A fast train is approaching and will not stop here.

PIP: Oh god it's so loud. I hate it here!

Oh! *Please* can you help me—

TRAIN STAFF MEMBER VOICEOVER: Can you keep back from the yellow line, love.

(PIP *reaches her limit and screams in frustration.*)

PIP: DON'T CALL ME LOVE! Ahhh! (*Throws possessions on floor.*) I wish everyone would just fuck off and leave me alone!!!!

JEAN: I think you should calm down, dear.

PIP: No, I will not calm down, Jean. I cannot calm down. I don't know how to calm down.

You know that.

Nobody else does. Why doesn't anybody else understand?

JEAN: Just tell them.

PIP: Why would I tell them? I don't even know them. They probably don't even know me. They probably don't even care about me. And you know what, I don't care about ANYTHING. I HATE CHANGE. I HATE TRAINS. I HATE SCHEDULES. AND I HATE THE WAY THAT TRAIN MAN SPOKE TO ME. And I know that I'm overreacting, but I CAN'T HELP IT!

JEAN: Oh, don't be so dramatic in front of these nice people.

(PIP *picks up textbook.*)

PIP: I'm not being dramatic, Jean. It's called 'Emotional Dysregulation'.

'This is an impaired ability to control your emotional response, leading to extreme or overblown reactions that don't really fit the situation. The intensity of these outbursts can rise so suddenly and significantly that they interfere with basic rationality.'

Last year I punched a bus stop because the bus didn't stop. And I once screamed and threatened to jump off a bridge because my housemate took my washing off the line when it was still damp. And once I was escorted out of the Victoria passport office by the security guard because I found the forms really overwhelming.

This book says there's a reason why I feel this anger and sadness so intensely and—

TRAIN TANNOY: Your attention please. This is a security announcement. Please do not leave your luggage unattended at the station. Luggage left unattended may be removed without warning or destroyed by the security services.

PIP (*overlapping the train tannoy*): AHH! Will you just let me talk? I'm trying to be real with them.

(PIP *realises she doesn't have her bag and runs around to find it.*)

What was I saying?

JEAN: I think you've forgotten, dear. I'm sorry I can't help you – all of a sudden there's absolutely nothing up here. It's like the bag you just left on the train. I am sorry. I don't know where those memories go, darling, but there's nothing here about them—

PIP: That's so weird. (PIP *picks up the textbook.*) 'If you aren't paying attention when you set something down, then your brain doesn't lay down a memory of the event.'

OK, that makes sense, but I do remember putting my bag in the overhead luggage.

JEAN: Yes, actually that is here, but then the memory suddenly... stops.

PIP: Maybe because I stopped looking at it.

JEAN & PIP (*realising*): Out of sight… out of mind. (*Laughter.*)

PIP: That makes so much sense! I never got that before.

But, it's not just me? Everyone forgets. (*Goes to textbook.*)

'Many symptoms of ADHD can be present in anyone's mind, but the difference for someone with ADHD is that their symptoms are constant and they can be so catastrophic or debilitating that they affect your everyday life.'

Yeah, so it's not helpful when someone says…

VERY POSH PERSON (PIP): I know how you feel. I lost my wallet. On the bus. It was about eight years ago now. Anyway, I think everyone has ADHD these days, don't they?

(*Slight pause.*)

TRAIN TANNOY: This is a security announcement. In the interests of safety, the riding of skateboards, rollerblades and cycles on this station is prohibited.

PIP (*to self, whilst looking up at the train board*): Platform ten, Edinburgh. OK! I'm on time. Phew, you've got this.

(PIP *puts on headphones just before the announcement says 'platform ten' and Mozart begins to play.*)

TRAIN TANNOY: Please may we have your attention. This is a platform alteration. If you are waiting on platform ten for the 11.20 service to Edinburgh please go to platform seven immediately as your train has been moved and is ready to depart.

Can any passengers waiting on platform ten please go to platform seven immediately to avoid missing the train to Edinburgh.

(PIP *has still not heard the announcements, and is swaying to the music while letting people around her step past.*)

TRAIN WORKER: Excuse me, love, if you're here waiting for the Edinburgh train, it's changed platforms. You've got about thirty seconds to catch it... Hello?

(PIP *is now dramatically conducting the music, pretending there is a full orchestra in front of her. Sound effects – train pulling away. Pause.*)

PIP (*removing her headphones*): I love Mozart! Many historians and medical professionals believe he had ADHD. I feel like I've spent this whole time talking about the negatives of ADHD, but so many creative, and successful, people have it... There's Geena Davis, Sue Perkins, Simone Biles...

JEAN: And Musicians! That Justin Timberlake, Mel B, Kerry Katona, Britney Spears!

PIP: Yes! I'm getting to them!

There's also actors like Liv Tyler, Emma Watson and Aisling Bea. And whilst I'm sure ADHD made things harder for them, it could have helped too, because there is one huge thing I've not told you about yet...

(*Spotlight on* PIP.)

AMERICAN COMMERCIAL VOICE (PIP): Are you one of the millions of people living with ADHD?

Do you struggle with focus, often finding yourself staring into the abyss...

Well, what if we told you that ADHD has a superpower? And it's called Hyperfocus.

(*Peppy commercial music starts.*)

Hyperfocus is the ability to become completely absorbed in a task.

It's like having a laser-sharp focus that can last for hours – even days!

Whether you're a student revising for exams – nice work, Billy! – or a scientist on the brink of a new discovery, Hyperfocus is here to help you.

In a world full of distractions, don't let ADHD hold you back.

It's time to embrace your hyperfocus and let it take you to places you never thought possible.

(*Voice becomes monotone and rapidly spoken.*)

Hyperfocus is a complementary and compulsory symptom of ADHD.

Side effects include forgetting the outside world, and ignoring basic human needs such as eating, drinking and going to the toilet. Results may vary and can include spending hours looking at any random assortment of online content, cutting the entire lawn with a pair of scissors, or spending three days learning to do a Rubik's cube instead of revising for your exams.

(PIP *rummages in her bag for a Rubik's cube. She sits and stares whilst finishing the cube.*)

PIP: Why do people call hyperfocus a superpower if you can't choose when to use it?

(*Holds up completed Rubik's cube.*) I'll add this to my CV, though.

(*Puts Rubik's cube back and pulls out a multicoloured costume skirt.*)

I forgot about this!

OK, so yes, hyperfocus hasn't helped me compose a symphony, become a CEO, or even revise for a single exam. But it has given me an amazing collection of fancy-dress costumes! I once spent the best part of a day painting my entire body orange with black stripes to look like a tiger at a music festival.

(*Dance music. Disco lights.* PIP *is dancing around the space.*)

DANCER 1: Oh my god. What is this? I've got orange all over me!

DANCER 2: Uhhhh! It's not just you! It's over everyone! It's orange paint! Where's it coming from?

PIP: Me! It's coming from me. I painted myself orange to look like a tiger.

DANCER 3: You're too much. You've literally covered everyone around you in orange paint. You've gotta stand at the back of the tent now, mate. Away from everyone.

(*Out to the front:*) This girl is so weird.

(PIP *moves to the back, keeping distance from everyone and saying 'sorry'. Dance music fades out, lights come up.*)

PIP (*to self*): It's just a festival, it doesn't matter.

JEAN: Yes, darling. Nothing really matters. Things like this always happen to you, and it's fine! You'll get over it soon.

PIP: Yeah, I know.

JEAN: It's just like when you bought those concert tickets for the wrong date. It was just one show, and you don't care about it now.

(*Being extra cheery as if this is her famous line:*) Because it doesn't matter!

PIP: Yeah. You're right, it was just a show. It doesn't matter.

JEAN: Or it's like when you bought tickets to that event in Birmingham. But they wouldn't let you in at the door, because the ticket's *you'd* purchased were for an event in San Francisco.

PIP: I did cry about that. But you're right, I'm over it now and it doesn't matter!

JEAN: Or when you were house-sitting and you left the keys two hours away...

PIP: I mean, that round trip cost me £80, but... No, no, I guess you're right. It's just money, it doesn't matter.

JEAN: Or when you misread the Edinburgh Fringe application deadline.

PIP: Yeah just a… actually, why are you bringing that up? That was really frustrating. I've had to wait a whole year!

JEAN: Or when you nearly killed a cat.

PIP: It survived!

JEAN: Or when you got distracted crossing the road.

PIP: I survived!

JEAN: Or when you had a panic attack in the library because you didn't understand the assignment.

(PIP *goes to speak, but the gaps close between* JEAN *'s sentences and they begin to overlap and spiral.*)

JEAN. Or when you left the gas on for four hours in someone else's house, and when they came home that night they nearly lit—

Or when you lied and said you could drive—

Or when you had sex with that man—

Or when you smashed that eighteenth-century rare china—

Or when you lost £300 because you forgot to close your—

Or when you cried in front of the customers—

Or when you threw that vase at the wall—

Or when the doctor diagnosed you with depression—

Or when you dropped your friend's phone in the toilet—

Or when you shouted at the man in—

Or when you broke the window of your friend's—

Or when you got caught with a—

Or when you forgot to call your mum and she—

Or when the nurse said you needed—

PIP: STOP!

(*Pause.* PIP *sits on a chair and talks to the* DOCTOR, *mirroring the earlier scene.*)

PIP: I've got ADHD?

Yeah, actually this makes a lot of sense.

These stupid things always happen to me.

I mean, I turn them into funny anecdotes. Like, I once had a bath in someone else's home, and managed to flood the house and blow the electrics!

It was so bad. I've told that story so many times I've nearly forgotten about the part when the owners came home.

I never tell that bit.

Because no one is going to laugh if I finish my story by telling them I had a panic attack.

Or that I cried at the end. Or that I made someone else cry.

I ruined someone's garden once, and I didn't go back. I didn't see the owner because I couldn't bear to see her reaction.

So many people probably think I'm rude or don't care because I don't listen or interrupt or make stupid choices.

I've hurt so many friends. I made my sister cry because she thought I didn't care.

My ex once got an Uber home in the middle of the night because I impulsively said something insensitive to her and I still to this day don't understand what I said wrong.

I don't mean to be like this, and it makes me feel really, really shit. But I don't know how to stop it.

(*Slight pause.*)

You think I should take medication?

Will that fix everything?

Will it change me?

(*Pause. Confident music starts.* PIP *gets up, walks about. Feeling good, different. People start saying things to her.*)

FRIEND: Wow, look at you. I've never seen you so determined!

TEACHER: Pip, I just want to say, well done on finishing your dissertation!

FRIEND: Hey, love, you're listening so well, and that's amazing... but you can say something too if you want to?

(*Music starts fading out.*)

FRIEND: Pip, you seem very quiet. Are you all right? I was thinking I could take you out and cheer you up over a beer?

PIP: Jean, what was that funny story about the beer? The one with the frozen... Jean?!

FRIEND: I'm really worried about you, Pip. You've been down for months. You seem like a completely different person. And you've stopped talking.

PIP: Jean?

Why is it so quiet?

TRAIN ANNOUNCEMENT: We are proud to welcome you to the new and exciting HS2. The elite and ultra-fast train. Cutting out the smaller trains. The complicated routes. This new train goes at top speed, directly through the country. Travel in peace and silence. With one route. One track. One train.

PIP: I want to get off!

(PIP *sits down and talks to the* DOCTOR.)

PIP: I think I want to stop the medication.

Because I feel really sad.

Yeah, I… Oh, um, yes, work is better.

Uh, yes my course is also going OK. Well, I finished my dissertation. But I can't…

Um, no, I haven't been making mistakes really, but…

I was trying to say I feel really sad. Um, I just don't feel like myself. I've never felt this way before – I don't really know how else to describe it, but…

(PIP *sits back, realising the* DOCTOR *is not listening to her.*)

PIP: He wasn't listening to me.

He wasn't even looking at me.

I'd lost over a stone since taking those tablets and he didn't notice.

He was only interested to know if I could function as a member of society in a neurotypical world.

But he didn't care if I could function as an actual person in MY world.

(*Slight pause.*)

Sorry, I'm meant to say something light-hearted now. But I don't have the words.

I just feel let down.

I *felt* let down by the doctor.

But I *feel* let down by the NHS. I feel let down by the whole system.

I feel let down by my teachers, my schools. I feel let down by the media, because they call ADHD a craze. I feel let down and I feel angry with the patriarchy because they told us ADHD was just for little boys. I feel angry with capitalism for convincing me what success is supposed to look like. I feel angry with the Tory government for not taking disabilities seriously and the mess they've left behind, and I feel angry with myself. Because I listened to everything. I just went along with it and believed everything was my fault because I was the problem. I believed I was naughty, I thought I was just a bit stupid. Attention-seeking, emotional, lazy, reckless, forgetful, unreliable – but I also believed that once I understood this, everything would get better.

(*Slight pause.*)

Well, everything is worse.

(*Slight pause.*)

(*Looking for* JEAN:) And I'm on my own now.

(PIP *starts to tidy up, putting various items into her backpack. On picking up the cucumber she holds it in the same way as in an early scene pretending it is a lawnmower handle. At this moment we hear* JEAN.)

JEAN: Helllooooooooooooo!

PIP: Jean? Jean?

Don't go!

I stopped the tablets months ago, but I didn't know if you'd come back…

JEAN: Ohh, don't be so dramatic in front of these nice people.

PIP: I'm not being dramatic!

JEAN: No one wants to hear something serious and personal.

PIP: Jean, stop!

That doesn't mean I want you to go.

I know now that I need you, but I also know that I need to talk. And I need to be able to finish a story. Will you let me finish this story?

(*Pause.*)

Where was I?

Ah yes.

I know medication is life-changing for a lot of people… but it didn't work for me. Maybe I could have tried a different dose, but the doctor didn't offer it to me. And honestly, I'd spent my whole life not being taken seriously. If things were going to change, they had to come from me.

I started exercising regularly, swimming, eating properly. I tried meditation, journalling and therapy.

Therapy was amazing. I learnt about my life, my past and why I am the way I am.

And then I went to group therapy and other people learnt about my life, my past and why I am the way I am.

Ten people sharing stories, with only ninety minutes. It was really hard to stay focused and keep to my time.

But in the end group therapy was more helpful than any of the other things I tried.

My mind had been quiet for a whole year. But saying everything out loud, to a room of complete strangers helped me realise that this is who I am!

(As soon as PIP *finishes speaking a train arrival ding sounds.* PIP *moves quickly around, gathering up all her belongings and all the props from the set as the conductor speaks.)*

TRAIN TANNOY: Good afternoon, this is your train driver speaking. We are now arriving into Edinburgh Waverley... Please check the overhead lockers for any personal items before disembarking this train. Thank you for travelling with First Great Western today, and we wish you a pleasant onward journey. Please mind the gap between the train and the platform edge as you alight from the train.

PIP: I hadn't realised we were already here! And I hadn't realised my stuff was everywhere. I've been running behind all morning. I missed the first train to Edinburgh because they changed the platforms, and no one told me! I'll be out of everyone's way in a second!

(PIP, *wearing backpack and holding bag, waits at train door, reaches into bag and pulls out phone.*)

PIP (*to self*): It was here the whole time!

WOMAN ON THE TRAIN: Helloooo?! Are you gonna press the button? We're here. Cor, you've got your head in the clouds!

PIP (*pushing the train door button*): I know!!

(*She steps forward off the train as 'ADHD' by Kara Marni plays. Lights go out.*)

THE END

ACKNOWLEDGEMENTS

The first draft of *Character Flaw* was written in 2021, but it wasn't until 2023, after family illness, that I realised how short life is, and if something is keeping you awake at night – you need to just do it!!

In 2021, during a particularly long and confusing train journey, I wrote the opening monologue. Which is why it is all about trains! The rest of the play I finished in five days at a friend's kitchen table, accompanied by Frankie the cat. Thank you to Lily and Alex for letting me use this space and for all your support. In 2023, Nat Kennedy brought the script to life through workshops and hours of play to find the fun and games in the words I had written. We both worked hard during a heatwave, rehearsing anywhere we could, to bring life to the script. I'm eternally grateful for the joy Nat brought to *Character Flaw*. Thank you also to their partner Blioux, who had to tiptoe around while we pushed their furniture to the walls and rehearsed for many hours in the sitting room.

Making a show about ADHD, when you have ADHD, comes with many challenges. I have been so lucky to have brilliant friends who have been supportive and encouraging during this whole process. I'm especially grateful to Andrea, Valentina, Ceri, Tash, Lucy and Lou. Emily for being my rock in Edinburgh, and to the Hereford Massive, always.

Claud Mayne designed the beautiful poster art and Josephine Li worked tirelessly to compose the music.

Character Flaw premiered at Edinburgh Festival Fringe in 2023 and was directed by Nat Kennedy.

The role of Pip was played by Philippa Dawson. The voice of Jean was read by Charly Clive, and the train tannoys and Amy were by Helen Colby. Matt Penman and Samuel Wightman read the male announcements.

The run exceeded all our expectations, selling out, recieving fantastic feedback and winning the Brighton Fringe Award for Excellence! The entire crew at Greenside were so supportive, especially the Nicolson Square team, who became like a family during those busy weeks. Thank you to Richard Jordan for recognising our story and putting us up for the Excellence Award!

I am grateful to every single person who has supported me on this journey. I'd especially like to thank the people who have been there, first-hand, through the stories in this play. My parents and my siblings Aubrey, Caroline and Justine – I am so lucky to be your little sister, and to have your endless support!

Thank you to my partner Jemima, who is currently driving me to Edinburgh as I write this! I feel so loved and lucky.

And finally thank you to Charlotte Amelia Poe – whose book *How to Be Autistic* inspired me more than they could know!